Divine Alliances

Prophetic Insight About Marriage,
Ministry, and Business Partnerships

Doug Addison

www.DougAddison.com

ISBN-13: 978-0-9824618-2-2

ISBN-10: 0-9824618-2-8

Printed in USA by
InLight Connection
PO Box 7049
Santa Maria, CA 93456

Cover design by Lai-Kit Chan

For ordering information contact:

InLight Connection
(800) 507-7853

www.DougAddison.com

Table of Contents

Chapter 1: A Change Coming to Marriages, Ministries, and Businesses

The Angelic Visitation

In 1991, I was so desperate to make sense of my life that I began seeking God for direction. I was 32 years old and had rededicated my life to Jesus Christ just a few years prior. I was part of a great church and was growing in my spiritual gifts and then my entire life derailed again.

I had returned to Christianity in 1988 after being heavily involved in drugs and the occult. My life changed for the better and I decided to marry the woman I had been dating for the previous five years. She was not a Christian and I ignored the wise advice from friends and family and married her anyway. After we married she became increasingly unhappy about my faith and the new direction that my life was going. To make a long story short, she started living with another man and I was heartbroken, looking to God for answers.

I had made several unsuccessful attempts to restore my marriage but it ended in divorce. Since she was now pregnant with another man's baby and living with him, I felt that things were final. I went through a lengthy time of healing and counseling and relied a lot on my friends at church.

During that period of healing, most of my time was spent at work during the day and studying the Bible on my lunch break and in the evenings. On weekends I would go to Bible studies, church services, and conferences. I was growing in my ability to hear the voice of God through the Holy Spirit.

I remember going to a Friday night service at a church in Vacaville, California. During worship I saw a picture in my mind of a beautiful stream of water flowing through a wooded area. It was so vivid that I knew it had to be a vision from God. Whenever I would close my eyes, even to this day, I can still see the stream of water and feel supernatural peace.

After praying about how to respond to the vision, I felt that God was directing me to go camping and spend some time alone with Him in the woods. I had a strong feeling in my spirit that God wanted to speak to me so I came prepared with my Bible, some study books, my writing notebook, and my guitar so I could worship.

I decided to go tent-camping alone in the great Redwood Forest of Big Sur on the coast of California. Early in the morning on July 6, 1991, I went for a hike in the woods to pray. As I walked and prayed and worshipped God, I came upon the exact stream of water that I had seen in the vision the week before. I was blown away by the experience. Before I could even enjoy the peaceful setting there came a sudden, startling presence of God. It was as if I had walked into a heat wave that felt like a mini electrical storm (it was a cool sunny day). I immediately went to my knees and was breathless as waves of God's presence washed over me.

I knew that there must be an angel right in front of me. I had never experienced anything like this. Though I did not see anything, I felt the presence of God and knew that the angel was about to speak to me. It was as if I could hear the angel's voice speak directly to my spirit (it's hard to describe unless you have experienced it). I began to say out loud the words that the angel was speaking to me. The words came so rapidly and spontaneously that it was obvious that I was not making it up myself. My entire body pulsated with God's love and presence.

The angel told me about my mother's upcoming death and instructed me to tell my stepfather to stay in church because he will remarry a godly woman. I was also told not to tell anyone about my experience until I had seen these things happen. The strange part about this prophetic word was that my Christian mother was alive and well and my stepfather was not a Christian and did not go to church at the time. I knew that in the future when I saw these three events occur, it would signify that the rest of the message I received would transpire.

After the experience I first ran to a pay phone and called my mother to see if she was all right. I did not mention the encounter I had just had, but I did pray with her. I went back to my campsite and over the next 24 hours I continued to receive visions and deeper insight into various verses of the Bible. God began to direct me to 1 Corinthians 7:29–30 regarding marriage and some future events that were going to happen.

I also received over a dozen words of knowledge that I took back to my church for our Sunday night service. All of the words of knowledge were accurate and several people were healed, including one person who was healed of partial deafness. This confirmed to me that the entire experience was from God and not Satan masquerading "as an angel of light" (2 Corinthians 11:14).

I did some further study and research, but for the most part I felt that the revelation I received was too much for me to comprehend at that point in my life. I felt God tell me to file it away and not talk to anyone about it until He told me to. I have to admit that it was frustrating for me not to talk about such a powerful experience. Other people I knew were allowed to write books about their supernatural encounters but I knew that it was not God's timing for it yet.

That was 1991. As it turned out, my mom became terminally ill a few years later. My stepfather gave his life to Jesus Christ in the process and he began going to church. After my mother's death in 1999, I was able to share with my stepfather the message about staying in church and that he would remarry. Five years later I was the best man in his marriage to a very godly widow from his church. As I watched his bride come down the aisle God spoke to me that it was now time to pull out the message from 1991, because He was about to do something radically new in the area of marriages, relationships, ministries, and business partnerships. He was going to realign things and bring about strategic alliances.

So I began studying the prophetic word I had received in 1991 from the angel. I wrote an article and placed it on my Web site and would occasionally speak about the experience at churches and conferences. Over the past few years I began seeing this prophecy unfold. This book is about the deeper insight I received about the entire experience and things that God has shown me since.

Understanding the message

When I received the angelic visitation in 1991, God spoke to me about a radical change coming in the area of marriages, relationships, ministries, and business partnerships. During my spiritual encounter I was directed to look in the Bible at 1 Corinthians chapter seven which deals with marriage and related issues. One area of this chapter that stood out was verses 29–31.

1 Corinthians 7:29–31 NIV *What I mean, brothers, is that the time is short. From now on those who have wives should live as if they had none; those who mourn, as if they did not; those who are happy, as if they were not; those who buy something, as if it were not theirs to keep; those who use the things of the world, as if not engrossed in them. For this world in its present form is passing away.*

The Apostle Paul writes "since the time is short," at first sight most people would think that he was referring to the second coming of Christ and that we need to be prepared. A deeper look at the actual Greek text reveals that "since the time is short" is translated from the Greek word, sunestalmenos, which is a common word used in sailing. It means to furl or contract a sail in order to withstand high winds and remain stable. Furling prevents a boat from capsizing or damaging the sails. Another way to look at this verse is in the context of the entire chapter as it pertains to marriage where Paul is encouraging us to narrow our focus to prevent shipwreck. Narrowing our focus means to not get distracted from the things that God calls us to accomplish. Another way to look at it is being single-minded.

God spoke to me specifically about these three verses and correlated them with a coming move of the Holy Spirit on the earth. A time is coming when things will not look as they normally do. For instance, Paul writes about men having a wife and living as though they had none. This does not mean that we live as if we are single, but rather that we are able to serve God together without getting entangled in the worries of life. Mourn as if you are not mourning, be happy as if you are not happy, buy things and not worry about owning them. This all sounds a bit contradictory but it actually means that the way things are usually done will radically change. In other words, the way we normally experience life will soon change and God is calling us to focus on His plan and purpose for our lives. As this new focus comes, many Christians will become much more effective in their ministries and businesses during this time.

Right now God is changing the attitudes of Christians everywhere, and a fresh strategy is being released from Heaven to establish a new major move of God bringing revival on earth. God will begin to supernaturally strengthen existing marriages and bring a new focus to couples to fulfill their ultimate destinies in God. He is also bringing together couples and their marriages will be centered upon a higher Kingdom purpose. The focus of these families will not be on earthly possessions and on traditional family life. God is calling families to become fully committed to their individual and collective callings in the Kingdom of God. This new focus and strategy from God will happen similarly in ministries and Christian-owned businesses. The right people will be brought together at the right time to create an effective release of anointing and finances.

As this change begins to happen, it will look strange to many people because age, race, and social background will not be a barrier to these marriages, ministries, and business partnerships. This new move from God will go beyond getting people to simply attend church services. Christians who have not seen themselves as going into ministry will come to the place where their entire life "is ministry." Many men and women have been single for a number of years because God has spared them from marrying someone who does not share the same calling and destiny. As God brings these new marriages together, many Christians will be quick to judge them because they will look quite strange to those without discernment. These new marriages, ministries and business teams will have a passion and singular focus.

To many people's surprise, existing marriages will be strengthened as well. Christians who have been married to an unbelieving spouse or to one who is more worldly-minded will suddenly find themselves with a new vision that they both agree with and are passionate about. Events will take place in families that will drive married couples closer. As God begins to increase this new anointing, unfortunately, some spouses will choose to leave the marriage. God will not force His will on anyone. It is never God's intention to cause divorce nor for a marriage to fall apart. However, it is inevitable that not everyone will respond to God in a positive way. For any marriage that does end in divorce, God is faithful and will restore those who seek Him.

Prodigal sons and daughters will return to God. Many children of Christian parents, particularly "Pastor's kids" will begin to get a new vision from God about their life. It will be as if a light was suddenly turned on and their life's purpose is revealed to them. In the parable about the Prodigal son in the New Testament, the older brother became jealous of the young son who came back home and was blessed by the father (Luke 15:28–32). In the same way, mature Christians will need to be careful not to judge or become jealous as these younger reignited Christians launch into great ministries with little effort.

A divine realignment will occur that brings couples together for the strategic purpose of God's Kingdom. Suddenly many people who were divorced or widowed will begin to remarry at an accelerated rate. Though divorce and death are not God's will, God will redeem them. In some cases it will appear as though some ministries are finished, but God will bring great surprises as He repays people for the years of suffering they have experienced. Those who focus on God will not miss His new purposes.

The Apostle Paul remarks throughout 1 Corinthians chapter seven that it is better to remain unmarried and serve the Lord. Similarly, God will bring couples together for His purposes so that there will be marriages that allow His servants to freely serve Him with greater impact as if they were single, yet they will be happily and firmly married. They will not get bound up with the cares of this world or focus on their own households; instead there will be incredible spiritual synergy that comes from being in agreement and together serving God with higher purposes. This does not mean that they will not own houses and raise families. Many will be blessed beyond their dreams. Finances will flow to them from many avenues which will allow them to fulfill all that God calls them to do.

Being single and staying pure is not an easy thing to do, especially with the added warfare that comes along with pursuing God's destiny for your life. The Apostle Paul encourages marriage if you burn with passion. It is better to marry than to fall to sexual sin (1 Corinthians 7:9). Many people need healing in the area of their sexuality. Assuming you have been healed of emotional hurts and dealt with generational sin issues in your life, passionate desire may very well be an indication that God is directing you towards marriage. Appropriate sexual intimacy within a marriage is powerful spiritual warfare. When two are joined together as one, the enemy has less of a chance to bring division and temptation. Walking this close together brings a greater prayer covering for each member of the couple. When you are one in the spirit you know how to pray for your spouse.

This new move of God will be comparable to the strategy in a game of chess. I saw in a vision a chessboard where the pieces were being moved into place. This represented God strategically realigning people. If you have ever played chess, you have to have a "bird's eye view" to see the big picture and the technique needed to get close to "The King." However, if you were actually one of the pieces on the chessboard it would be difficult to see the next move or what God is doing in your life. As God realigns these relationships it will go beyond ministry and flow into business as well. Many couples are being called by God to strategically supply finances to further God's work on earth through businesses.

Doug Addison

Chapter 2: A New Paradigm for Christians

God strengthening marriages

It is easy to see that Christianity has somehow lost its effectiveness and appeal in the new millennium. The fact remains that God is still God, and His love, power, and acceptance are available to everyone. Biblical Christianity goes deeper than the Christianity that is typically seen today. It is as if today's style of Christianity is fulfilling the words of Jesus to the Church of Laodicea in Revelation 3:14–22 where the condition of that church was lukewarm. He went on to say that although they thought they were rich, in His eyes they were "wretched, pitiful, poor, blind, and naked." It is easy to see that many Christians are lukewarm. If we are in this condition spiritually, I certainly pray that God will heal and restore us.

We need a new paradigm for the way we live and understand Christianity. This new standard is what I saw coming in the spiritual experience and visitation I had in 1991, and it's something radical that will allow us to get into sync with God's desires for this generation. When I first began sharing this with others in 2004, many Christians misunderstood what I was saying and began focusing on one aspect of the message, particularly the part about divorce. They quickly dismissed what I said because it could not be from God if divorce was involved.

I want to clarify that God will not cause divorce to bring about this realignment. Divorce happens because of the attack of Satan against marriages. God will take what was intended for evil and turn it around for good (Genesis 50:20). God wants to strengthen existing marriages. He wants to prevent divorce. However, if you or someone you know has suffered in this area, God will redeem you if you seek Him for restoration.

People may try to take a message like this one to justify getting out of a marriage in which they are not happy. It is not my intention to judge anyone. I will refrain from commenting on specific situations and let it be between you and God. My prayer is that marriages will be strengthened to a level not seen before. Only God knows your situation and your heart. Let Him speak to you and guide you through your times of trouble.

Equally yoked

There are a large number of what we refer to as "unequally yoked" marriages in churches today. This phrase is from 2 Corinthians 6:14, in which one spouse is a dedicated Christian and the other is not. I want to encourage you to stay married and pray for your spouse if at all possible.

1 Corinthians 7:26–28 *Are you married? Do not seek a divorce. Are you unmarried? Do not look for a wife.*

If you are single and considering marrying an unbeliever or a person who does not have the same commitment to Christ as you do, I want to caution you that you may not have the same level of effectiveness in the Kingdom of God that you would if you marry a person who shares your vision and can provide help and encouragement.

Ecclesiastes 4:9 *Two are better than one, because they have a good return for their work ...*

If you are considering marrying an unbeliever, talk first to others you know who have done the same. Or do an internet search on the phrase 'unequally yoked' and read some of the stories of people who thought they would be happy with their marriage but had to sacrifice a huge part of their faith. There will most likely be pain involved eventually. Again, it is between you and God. In the past I have suffered from being in a marriage with a person who did not share my beliefs. Somehow I thought I could change my ex-wife but it did not turn out the way I had hoped. My "unequally-yoked" marriage ended tragically and it was a very painful period of my life. I learned a lot about God's forgiveness and mercy in the process. I have since recovered and I am blessed to be in an "equally-yoked" marriage now. My earlier marriage and subsequent pain would have been prevented had I heeded the warnings of those around me.

The strategic marriages I saw in the vision were couples coming together; two believers working towards a common vision for God's Kingdom. You cannot design it on your own. God will create it but it will require some effort on your part to respond when it happens. It will require you to trust Him and to say yes when the opportunity comes along.

I don't want to discourage you if you are currently married to someone who does not share your same faith or passion for God. My advice is to stay married and pray that your spouse will respond as God reveals Himself to them. It is possible to still have a happy marriage with an unbeliever. As well, it is possible that God called you to marry the person you are with. It is also still possible for you as a believer to have a successful life and ministry while being married to an unbeliever. I am not trying to judge anyone's situation.

My point is that there would be a greater effectiveness in the Kingdom of God if the majority of couples were together for the single focused purpose of ministry. Over the past decades this has been the opposite. Most people are not aware of many powerful spiritual principles from the Bible that apply to relationships and marriage. There are many key elements in the Bible that define a marriage that is fulfilling God's purposes.

Being in agreement is a very powerful spiritual principle that releases synergy. Synergy is where two or more combined forces have a much greater impact than they would separately. There are many verses in the Bible about this concept. Deuteronomy 32:30 describes a principle where one person can chase away 1,000 and two can put 10,000 to flight. How much more effective are two people serving God together? It's an exponential increase in effectiveness!

Matthew 18:19 *"Again, I tell you that if two of you on earth agree about anything you ask for, it will be done for you by my Father in heaven. ..."*

Importance of non-abusive relationships

Many gifted men and women of God are currently being held back from their callings by abusive spouses and marital relationships. Abuse should never be tolerated. Some people have suffered abuse and are now divorced and living their life single. As God calls couples together for His purposes, it will require trusting and getting healed of the wounds and emotional hurts that your abusive marriage brought to you. It was never God's will for you to suffer abuse. The fact that Satan worked overtime trying to hold you back is an indicator that you have a call and destiny from God for something great!

Ephesians 5:25 *Husbands, love your wives, just as Christ loved the church and gave himself up for her.*

Many women today have been so wounded by men that they now can only trust God. I often hear women say, "Jesus is my husband." This is a great commitment to make, and is sincere when it is God calling you to do this. However, make sure you are not using this as a cover-up for unhealed wounds and unforgiveness. This can go for men as well as women. It is more difficult for a man to see God as a spouse-replacement. We need each other in the church today. Trust can and must be restored to live a healthy, balanced spiritual life.

Some people choose to relate primarily to God because they have been wounded by other people. Then there are those who can only relate to themselves because they lack the ability to trust God and others. And then there are people who can relate to other people more than to themselves or God. They have been so wounded that they lack self-esteem. A healthy, balanced life allows us to relate to ourselves, other people, and to God in a balanced way. If you fall into any of these categories, I highly encourage you to get prayer or counseling to help bring healing and balance to your life.

Biblical principle of a spiritual covering

Many women have been filling positions in the Kingdom of God and doing a great deal of work. I want to commend women for their hard work and passion for Jesus Christ.

Unfortunately, because of spiritual abuse and discrimination against women, this idea of a "spiritual covering" for many people might be unclear or associated with a bad experience. When church leaders rely on a woman to lead or fill a position, but they do not give them the authority they need to do it, they are not providing a true spiritual covering. This is the same in the business world.

God designed men and women—the masculine and feminine—to operate together in unity. What one lacks, the other is able to provide. This goes both ways, for men as well as women. For women to step into the higher levels of authority that God is calling them to, they need to be given authority and support. This covering comes from a husband, a pastor, or a leader (it does not have to be from a man). Currently things are out of alignment in this area.

God will move to provide marriages for a great number of single men and women in the Church who are seeking His will and divine purpose for their lives. When this strategy begins to come into place, husbands and wives will begin to cover each other in prayer and support that will bring a new balance into the Kingdom of God.

Acts 2:17–18 *"In the last days, God says, I will pour out my Spirit on all people. Your sons and daughters will prophesy, your young men will see visions, your old men will dream dreams. Even on my servants, both men and women, I will pour out my Spirit in those days, and they will prophesy ..."*

As couples come together as one, their ministries, gifts, anointing, and businesses will accomplish beyond the extent of what they would have been able to achieve separately. The order of things is about to be reversed. Instead of seeing a large number of unequally-yoked marriages, we will see a larger number of equally-yoked marriages.

Bringing together strategic gifting and callings

Mark 10:7–8 *'For this reason a man will leave his father and mother and be united to his wife and the two will become one flesh' So they are no longer two, but one.*

God is strategically aligning people's gifts and ministry callings. This will include businesses as well. There is power in combining the calling and resources of two people. Isaiah 11:2 gives a description of several aspects of the Spirit of the Lord:

- The Spirit of wisdom and of understanding
- The Spirit of counsel and of power
- The Spirit of knowledge and of the fear of the Lord

Notice they are mentioned in pairs. By strategically pairing gifts and callings, God will take the effectiveness of one ministry's calling and increase it dramatically. In some cases a husband or wife can take on a support role for the one who has a ministry calling with a higher impact. Others will operate as a ministry team. You can see this concept in Luke 10:1 as Jesus sent out seventy-two of His disciples to minister. He sent them in teams of two.

Making sacrifices and providing stability so that another person may serve God is powerful as well. Not all ministry couples will share the role of being in front of people. My wife provides an emotional support that I lacked for years to be able to fulfill my higher calling. Though she is not up front ministering with me, she brings wisdom. I tend to operate in understanding the bigger picture of how things fit together. She has counsel and I operate in power. There are many other areas as well that we complement each other's gifts. It is a match that could not have been made by any dating service.

I know a man in ministry who became widowed a few years ago. God brought a woman to him who is much younger than he. She had been divorced years ago and was waiting for God to bring a new marriage to her. Their marriage is a Divine Alliance. As they came together their marriage was for the purposes of ministry and expanding God's Kingdom. She is an intercessor and gets words of knowledge and he has a prophetic gift. They minister together. As he teaches she gets words of knowledge for ministering to people and for his writing. Not all marriages will function this way, but there will be a dramatic increase in ones that will over the next few years.

Why some remain single

Many people have been promised by God that they would be brought the right mate to help them serve God for the rest of their lives. God promised me a wife who would help balance me. When I met my wife, she had a promise from God that her future husband would be like the "missing wheel to her car." My gifts provide the balance that she needs to fulfill her calling.

To some it may seem like God has forgotten about His promise for the right marriage for you. In reality God is lining things up and wants the best for you. Timing is everything. God does not want you to suffer or perish. He does not want you to settle for less. Wait on Him and in time He will give you all that he has promised to you.

2 Peter 3:8–9 *But do not forget this one thing, dear friends: With the Lord a day is like a thousand years, and a thousand years are like a day. The Lord is not slow in keeping his promise, as some understand slowness. He is patient with you, not wanting anyone to perish, but everyone to come to repentance.*

Some people are remaining single because they gave up looking for someone. There is a spiritual principle found in Matthew 7:7–8:

"Ask and it will be given to you; seek and you will find; knock and the door will be opened to you. For everyone who asks receives; he who seeks finds; and to him who knocks, the door will be opened."

God can bring a relationship to you but if you never leave your house you might be missing opportunities. I remember when God restored me from divorce. I went through some counseling and read some books and began to feel better about myself. I went on a few dates because I was trying to learn a new behavior of recognizing healthy and unhealthy relationships. When I was single I wanted to know what a healthy marriage looked like, because there was a great deal of divorce in my family. I would go to friends of mine who had a good marriage and hang out with them, observing their relationship while asking God to help me to get to that place someday.

Others remain single because God has truly called them to do this. It is a great and noble commitment. I want to honor those of you who are like the Apostle Paul who felt it was best to remain single. You will experience a great renewal in this move of God as well. There will be Divine Alliances that come in the form of ministries and businesses that will help strengthen and support you to fulfill all that God has called you to as well.

Prophetic words to marry someone specific and Soul Mates

Sometimes we need to wait for the one that God has promised us. On the other hand there are people who have received promises from God to marry a specific person. This is not always easy to understand. Anytime we hear a personal prophetic word from God, it is situational and subjective. One example from the Bible is when Jonah brought a prophetic word of destruction to Nineveh. They repented and God did not bring the destruction that the prophet had prophesied. In the same way, if God has told you that you will marry a specific person, be sure to understand that the other person has the opportunity to say yes or no. God will not force Himself on anyone. It might have been God's intention and desire for you to marry that person but if they say no, then that word is void. You can be sure that God will bring someone else that is perfect for you.

People ask me often about the idea of soul mates. They feel that there is someone out there and that when they meet someone that seems special, they wonder—is this my soul mate? The notion of a soul mate was made popular over two thousand years ago by the Greek philosopher Plato. He surmised that a perfect human being was tragically split in two, resulting in a race of creatures sentenced to spend the rest of their lives searching for that missing "other" who can complete them.

I don't agree with the philosophy and it is definitely not a Biblical principle. We do not need another person to make ourselves whole. It is God who makes us an integrated person. God can bring us the perfect mate. In marriage, God said two become one but that doesn't mean we are halves without our spouse. We are formed into a unit that is spiritual. Unfortunately, many people today are emotionally and relationally damaged. Oftentimes they seek out the wrong type of person that reinforces their wounded soul.

If there is a history in your life or in your family of divorce, incest, abuse, or adultery, then I highly recommend some type of emotional healing sessions, prayer ministry, or seminars to help rid you of the tentacles of these dark forces.

Understanding death

Death is often misunderstood and even feared. If you have given your life to God through Jesus Christ, there really is no need to fear death. Our life on earth is just the beginning of an eternal life in Heaven. For those who have experienced suffering or watched your loved ones suffer, it is comforting to view death as the ultimate healing.

Unless you have been through it, the premature death of a spouse is difficult to understand. William Branham, one of the greatest prophets that lived during the 1950s Healing Movement, lost his wife and baby girl early in his ministry. He had a visitation from God in which he was shown that they were doing great in Heaven. It helped him with his grief and allowed him to feel released to remarry.

My mother died after suffering several years from brain tumors and other related diseases. As she lay on her bed in hospice care, I still remember her murmuring the words

"Praise the Lord" all the way until the end when she couldn't speak. My mom was a woman of great faith and compassion and she is now in Heaven praying for me I'm sure.

Psalm 116:15 *Precious in the sight of the Lord is the death of his saints.*

Hebrews 12:1 *Therefore, since we are surrounded by such a great cloud of witnesses, let us throw off everything that hinders and the sin that so easily entangles, and let us run with perseverance the race marked out for us.*

Sometimes when a person dies it causes a chain reaction in the spirit after they are gone. The gifts and callings that they had in their life may appear to fall to the ground, but in the spiritual realm they are actually available and imparted to others. There are things that our ancestors were called by God to do, whether they were Christians or not. And if they did not fulfill their calling, then it is available to us to ask God if we can pick up their calling. My great-grandfather was a traveling lay-preacher in the Appalachian Mountains. This calling to travel and spread the good news of Jesus was not picked up by his son or my father. I am now fulfilling that calling.

John 12:24 *I tell you the truth, unless a kernel of wheat falls to the ground and dies, it remains only a single seed. But if it dies, it produces many seeds.*

Death is not easy to deal with and God is close to widows and the orphans. Here are few more verses from the Bible regarding death.

1 Thessalonians 4:13–14 *Brothers, we do not want you to be ignorant about those who fall asleep, or to grieve like the rest of men, who have no hope. We believe that Jesus died and rose again and so we believe that God will bring with Jesus those who have fallen asleep in him.*

2 Corinthians 5:8 *We are confident, I say, and would prefer to be away from the body and at home with the Lord.*

A word about divorce

The Divine Alliances that God showed me were between people who had gone through a lot of difficult times before they met each other. Some had battled to stay married, then had gone through divorce and God had brought a new spouse; still others were widowed, having lost their spouse through death. I saw God begin to bring together these types of people as couples who would have a single focus and a purpose of expanding God's Kingdom. I mentioned previously that some people will misunderstand this prophetic word and think that I am saying it is okay to divorce. Or they will use this as an excuse to get out of a marriage they do not like. I want to clarify that God is the one who is orchestrating Divine Alliances.

This prophetic word should not be used as a tool to divorce or encourage divorce. The fact is, divorce has bad consequences and is devastating for children, because it destroys their foundation and understanding of love and security. At the same time, I am not judging anyone who is divorced. I believe that God can heal and restore anything and anyone. I know firsthand because I have been divorced and my mother divorced my father when I was five years old.

Divorce is not an "unpardonable sin." God will forgive you and restore you no matter what— just look to His unfailing compassion and love. There is a lot of controversy among Christians regarding divorce. Some say that you can never be a minister after you divorce. Others say you will never have the ministry or impact that God intended before you divorced. I disagree with these points of view. God can and will forgive anything of your past. (1John 1:9) You may need to take time to get healed and restored to stability, but God will do it.

The saddest outcome of divorce is the emotional impact on children. As a five-year-old I did not understand why we had to leave Daddy. My mother remarried a great man when I was eight and to this day I cherish his relationship with me as much as my own father's. It took me years to unravel the negative impact my family's divorce had on me. I did not realize it until later in life that this caused me to have difficulty with trust and love.

Often, we view our relationship with our Heavenly Father through the filter of our experiences with our earthly parents. I honor parents and do not wish to disrespect them at all; I am a parent myself. Divorce can taint our view of God. We can covertly have issues of trust or think that God is mean, when in reality God is love.

Chapter 3: Strategic Plans for God's Kingdom

Develop a positive Kingdom mindset

Years after my initial angelic visitation in 1991, I received the following revelation about the Christian life. I thought that it would be helpful to mention it here because it can help move you towards your destiny much more quickly. The Divine Alliances that I saw being formed were meant to get people operating at a higher level in the spirit and in their own maturation.

Understanding God's Kingdom requires us to have spiritual eyes and ears. Jesus said over fifteen times that we must have "eyes that see and ears that hear." In John 5:19 (NLT) Jesus said, "... [I do] only what I see the Father doing." Notice the words "see" and "do". Not only do we need to see what God is doing but we also must be "doers of the word as well" (James 1:22 KJV).

Knowing God's intention for a situation allows us to be in agreement with Him. Sometimes it may be opposite from what we expect. Notice that Noah built an Ark in a dry season and Joseph advised Pharaoh to store up grain in a time of prosperity so that he would be a blessing in a time of famine. Not to mention all the spiritual principles that seem to be backwards from our natural thinking, things like: you must give to receive, the last will be first, if you humble yourself God will lift you up, etc.

The *Divine Alliances* that are coming may not all look nice, neat and orderly. They will not violate any principles of the Bible, but God is about to do some radical things to bring about a radical change in His Kingdom on earth. This will help us to fulfill our destinies at a level we have not seen before. Right now many Christians do not know what their destiny is. Many do not know their spiritual gifts or what God has called them to do.

1 John 4:4 tells us that the Spirit within us is greater than the one in the world around us (my paraphrase). Science has discovered that there is a major difference between light and dark. Light can be measured and it has substance and mass. Darkness, however, is simply the absence of light. Jesus is Light and Paul encourages us to live as children of Light. (Ephesians 5:8). Living our lives with a greater measure of God's love and light is extremely powerful. We then dispel darkness wherever we go. As Christians, we need to understand and regularly practice positive spiritual principles of praying for those who curse us, loving those who hate us, giving to those in need, helping the oppressed, being humble as opposed to proud and arrogant, forgiving those who offend us … the list is actually too long to expound on here but you get the picture. Notice that most of these principles are relationally oriented and they direct us on how to relate with others as opposed to just relating to God.

Many Christians love God but when no one is looking, they are guilty of mistreating people. We can change the spiritual atmosphere around us by loving, blessing, and being an encouragement. Here's the fun part: if you do these things regularly, the principle of sowing and reaping will eventually kick in. Your life will be overflowing with good things, to the point that you cannot help but change the world around you. What you sow is what you will reap. If you sow grumbling, doubt, fear, depression, anxiety, and complaining, then that is what you will get in return. Developing a positive Kingdom perspective and lifestyle is what will truly change our lives and the lives of many around us.

We need new strategies to bring God's love to a hurting world. We need some fresh and original ideas in churches, businesses, education, government, media, and all aspects of life. *Divine Alliances* will bring this about in an accelerated process.

The prayer David should have prayed

Getting to our destiny will require getting creative and finding ways to break through the things that have stopped us in the past. A great example of someone in the Bible who went through a difficult time but still fulfilled his destiny is David.

David was known as a man after God's own heart. He was not perfect but he did everything with gusto. At one point in King David's life, he got bored and had an affair with a beautiful woman named Bathsheba. She became pregnant and David had her husband killed as part of a cover-up. God revealed David's hidden sin through Nathan the prophet. When Nathan corrected David he said something very interesting that I have often thought would have been a key to preventing David's situation entirely.

2 Samuel 12:7–8 *"… (Nathan speaking) This is what the Lord, the God of Israel, says: 'I anointed you king over Israel, and I delivered you from the hand of Saul. I gave your master's house to you, and your master's wives into your arms. I gave you the house of Israel and Judah. And if all this had been too little, I would have given you even more."*

God was telling David that if he wanted more than God had already given him, all he had to do was ask to be fulfilled in another way, instead of taking it unlawfully. I believe this is the kind of prayer our Heavenly Father wants from us - to pray in a way that we are able to pour out our hearts in total honesty and wait on God to give us things in His timing. This is especially true if there are deep needs and desires we have that we feel are not being fulfilled. This is not just sexually, but in all areas of our lives. If we ask God and wait on Him, He will answer us—but the answer may not come in the way we think it will.

I often wonder what would have happened in David's life had he asked God for what he needed during that time of his life. We need to get this revelation in our lives that God cares so much about us that we can be brutally honest with Him. After all, He is the one who created us.

Our children are our destiny

The later result of David's sin with Bathsheba was a marriage that eventually brought a child into the world who would construct the Temple that David had set out to build. Solomon was part of David's destiny. This also shows that God will restore the things that the enemy intended for evil and use them for good. For those who have children, often we can get so focused on our own careers and spiritual life that we may not realize that our children are our ultimate destiny. With the right coaching and guidance they can achieve much more than we could ever accomplish in our own lives. Somehow, grandparents grasp this more than parents.

Isaiah 44:3–4 *I will pour out my Spirit on your offspring, and my blessing on your descendants. They will spring up like grass in a meadow, like poplar trees by flowing streams.*

A very powerful kingdom strategy is to help our children fulfill their own destiny. Sadly, the statistics show that the majority of children who grow up going to church never return after they move from their parent's home. This should be alarming to us and cause us to make a concerted effort to find out where we are going wrong. Why are our children not interested in church? I believe that this young generation has such a high destiny and calling from God that they will experience opposition. Most kids who leave church don't really have a problem with Jesus but somehow were not able to make the connection with their parents' God.

This generation is looking for something very real. They must believe in what they do with all their hearts or they are not interested at all. Most Sunday schools and youth groups are not providing the connection and challenge that they need. Music and expression of who they are play a big role in young people's culture. They want to be understood and unique so they have special ring tones on their cell phones, songs on their MySpace.com profiles, tattoos, and piercings.

The best way to help our children is to listen to them. Ask them specific questions about how they feel. Ask them to describe a type of church that they would like to attend. Help identify things that they are good at. These talents are often clues about their destiny. Do their friends open up and share their problems to them a lot? Then they probably have a strong gift of counsel. Do they give freely to people in need? Then they may have a gift of compassion. Are they strongly opinionated and seem to buck the system? Most likely they are a leader in the making.

My 24-year-old daughter was having difficulty deciding what she wanted to do with her life. I wanted her to pursue a higher vocation than she was in because of her intellect. She is smart, witty, and has a lot to give. I started to point out the things that I noticed she is good at. I helped her to recognize her strengths and helped her see the God-given gifts within her. I also agreed to help her in any way I could and let her know that I would support and bless her in whatever field she decided to pursue. Within a short period of time, she began to get a clearer picture of what she likes and wants to do and it was more suited to her intellectual level.

Our children are our destiny! It helps to see that they are not only the future generation, but that they can contribute now. We need to help them find new hope and purpose. Learn to speak their language, value their music, and talk about their problems - just to name a few things we can try.

Kingdom business strategies

Just as marriages will strengthen and couples will be brought together strategically, God is going to bring about a move of His Holy Spirit in the business world. Many Christian businessmen and women will begin to operate in a greater level of effectiveness. Until recently, anointed business people have not been completely understood by most Christians.

God will begin to pull together new Divine Alliances of gifting and strategy for the purpose of making money for Kingdom ministry. Inventions, ideas, and creativity are being released from Heaven not only for finances, but to evangelize world leaders in every sector: entertainment, business, education, government. Also the Church itself will find new strategies for doing church services and reaching "unchurched" people. The development of "for profit" businesses that will fund "not for profit" ministries and outreaches will increase and multiply.

I know of a church that had a difficult time paying their pastor. After considerable prayer, they recognized that there were not any burrito shops in their neighborhood. They opened a small "burrito to go" shop and made such a great return that not only were they able to pay their own pastor, but they started supporting missionaries. Another church opened a combination Christian bookstore and high-quality coffee shop franchise in their town. This allowed them to do evangelism and make a profit as well.

Be sure to check with your tax consultant about laws regarding non-profit organizations. This concept of creating profit from the business world to benefit God's people is in the Bible in the story of Joseph in Genesis 41:28–36. Pharaoh has two dreams about seven years of plenty that will be followed by seven years of famine. Joseph interprets the dreams of a world leader who was not a believer in Jehovah God. Joseph goes on to give Pharaoh advice on how to respond, "Store up grain in the time of plenty and sell it to the world in the time of famine." The result was that Joseph got out of prison and was placed as second in command in Egypt. Israel was spared from starvation due to the famine and they were brought to Egypt. It was during a big famine and economic downturn that Israel received new clothes, houses and gold!

Many people today are referring to this as a "Joseph anointing." This is the ability to hear God's voice and put plans into place to bring about great blessings. There are many Josephs—both male and female—who are about to come on the scene and be part of *Divine Alliances* in the business world.

It is interesting to note that Pharaoh had the dream, not Joseph. God gave the dream to Pharaoh but did not give him the understanding to fulfill it. This set the scene for one of God's people to show God's ultimate power to a world leader. Divine Alliances will positively influence world leaders and heads of state. How would we in the Church today view it if we saw a Christian businessman like Joseph working for an unbelieving world leader like Pharaoh? My guess is we wouldn't think it was a Divine Alliance! This makes my point that God will do something so radical it might be hard to see it's from God.

God will strategically align Christian business people together with the right mix of gifts. Separately they could not do what they could do together. As I said before, this is spiritual synergy. It will look strange to many Christians who do not have spiritual discernment to recognize that it is actually a movement from God. The spirit of poverty and lack of finances will be broken from the Church in such a way that it will cause the world to take note. These new financial blessings will not be used to build individual churches and ministries like we see today. Instead there will be Divine Alliances that will strategically use buildings, resources, people, and finances for a higher purpose. It will be to advance the Kingdom of God and usher in a new revival that has not been seen since the Book of Acts in the Bible.

Conclusion

I wrote this small book as a response to God's direction for me to do so. The message will build over time and you will begin to notice more and more of these Divine Alliances around you and you will not become a roadblock to family and friends who are called to these new types of relationships. I have already begun to see a great number of them over the past few years. There are many stories to share about how God is strengthening marriages, and how He is bringing healing and new marriages to those who have been divorced and widowed. Many prodigal sons and daughters are beginning to come back to Christ and to pursue their callings. There are businesses being formed and new strategies being released.

This is all designed to expand the Kingdom of God on earth. God is setting the scene for a huge realignment that will cause our efforts to become very successful and productive for God. My prayer is that this prophetic insight will encourage you in some way or maybe help someone you know. If it has, please let us know by going to the contact page on my Web site www.dougaddison.com. Please send us your stories and testimonies of how God has done this for you.

May God richly bless all that you do!

Doug Addison

Other Resources from Doug Addison

Kingdom Financial Strategies
2 CD Audio Set & Study Guide
Doug Addison uncovers many financial principles of which most people are unaware. As you apply these principles to your life you will begin to experience lasting change in the area of money, ministry, and business.

Accelerating Into Your Life's Purpose
10 Audio CDs & 62 page Journal
Discover your destiny, awaken passion, and transform your life with this 10 day interactive program. Designed to reveal your life's desires, remove obstacles, and create a written plan for what to focus on next.

Prophecy, Dreams, and Evangelism: *Revealing God's Love through Divine Encounters*
Book & Study Guide
Imagine what could happen if we could hear and speak what is on God's heart for individuals. The book & study guide are for everyone who longs to reach others with God's love in a relevant way.

For more information visit

www.dougaddison.com or call (800) 507-7853